How IT Managers Can Make Innovation Happen

Tips And Techniques For IT Managers To Use In Order To Make Innovation Happen In Their Teams

"Practical, proven techniques that will show you how to help your team to make innovation happen for them"

Dr. Jim Anderson

Published by:
Blue Elephant Consulting
Tampa, Florida

Copyright © 2013 by Dr. Jim Anderson

All rights reserved. No part of this book may be reproduced of transmitted in any form or by any means, electronic or mechanical, including photocopying, recording or by any information storage and retrieval system without written permission of the publisher, except for inclusion of brief quotations in a review.

Printed in the United States of America

Library of Congress Control Number: 2013923022

ISBN-13: 978-1494703479

ISBN-10: 1494703475

Warning – Disclaimer

The purpose of this book is to educate and entertain. This book does not promise or guarantee that anyone following the ideas, tips, suggestions, techniques or strategies will be successful. The author, publisher and distributor(s) shall have neither liability nor responsibility to anyone with respect to any loss or damage caused, or alleged to be caused, directly or indirectly by the information contained in this book.

Recent Books By The Author

Product Management

- Product Management Secrets: Techniques For Product Managers To Boost Product Sales And Increase Customer Satisfaction

- Customer Lessons For Product Managers: Techniques For Product Managers To Better Understand What Their Customers Really Want

Public Speaking

- How To Give A Great Presentation: Presentation techniques that will transform a speech into a memorable event

- How To Rehearse In Order To Give The Perfect Speech: How to effectively rehearse your next speech to that your message be remembered forever!

CIO Skills

- What CIOs Need To Know About Working With Partners: Techniques For CIOs To Use In Order To Be Able To Successfully Work With Partners

- How CIOs Can Make Innovation Happen: Tips And Techniques For CIOs To Use In Order To Make Innovation Happen In Their IT Department

IT Manager Skills

- Secrets Of Effective Leadership For IT Managers: Tips And Techniques That IT Managers Can Use In Order To Develop Leadership Skills

- IT Manager Career Secrets: Tips And Techniques That IT Managers Can Use In Order To Have A Successful Career

Negotiating

- Learn The Skill Of Exploring In A Negotiation: How To Develop The Skill Of Exploring What Is Possible In A Negotiation In Order To Reach The Best Possible Deal

- Learn How To Argue In Your Next Negotiation: How To Develop The Skill Of Effective Arguing In A Negotiation In Order To Get The Best Possible Outcome

Miscellaneous

- Power Distribution Unit (PDU) Secrets: What Everyone Who Works In A Data Center Needs To Know!

- Making The Jump: How To Land Your Dream Job When You Get Out Of College!

Note: See a complete list of books by Dr. Jim Anderson at the back of this book.

Acknowledgements

Any book like this one is the result of years of real-world work experience. In my over 25 years of working for 7 different firms, I have met countless fantastic people and I've been mentored by some truly exceptional ones. Although I've probably forgotten some of the people who made me the person that I am today, here is my attempt to finally give them the recognition that they so truly deserve:

- Thomas P. Anderson
- Art Puett
- Bobbi Marshall
- Bob Boggs

Dr. Jim Anderson

This book is dedicated to my wife Lori. None of this would have been possible without her love and support.

Thanks for the best 21 years of my life (so far)...!

Table Of Contents

LIGHTING THE SPARK OF INNOVATION IS PART OF BEING A SUCCESSFUL IT MANAGER 8

ABOUT THE AUTHOR 10

CHAPTER 1: IS AN IT MANAGER REALLY AN ARTIST? 15

CHAPTER 2: HOW IT LEADERS CAN GROW GOOD IDEAS 19

CHAPTER 3: 3 REASONS INNOVATION DOESN'T HAPPEN IN IT 22

CHAPTER 4: IT TAKES A VILLAGE TO INNOVATE LIKE AN IT DEPARTMENT 26

CHAPTER 5: DOING MORE WITH WHAT YOU ALREADY HAVE 30

CHAPTER 6: HOW SEEING THE FUTURE HELPED NCR'S IT LEADERS DO MORE 34

CHAPTER 7: THE REASON THAT INNOVATION ISN'T HAPPENING IN YOUR IT TEAM 38

CHAPTER 8: HOW IT MANAGERS CAN BRING INNOVATION TO THEIR IT TEAMS 42

CHAPTER 9: HOW IT MANAGERS CAN FIND THE INNOVATION THAT THEIR IT TEAMS NEED 46

CHAPTER 10: 3 STEPS IT MANAGERS CAN TAKE TO MAKE INNOVATION HAPPEN FOR THEIR TEAM 50

CHAPTER 11: HOW CAN IT MANAGERS BE INNOVATIVE? 54

CHAPTER 12: WHAT IF ANOTHER IT MANAGER JUST COPIED YOUR GREAT INNOVATIVE IDEA? 58

Lighting The Spark Of Innovation Is Part Of Being A Successful IT Manager

Every company wants to grow and become more successful. There is no magic formula to make this happen, but it is generally agreed that in order for this to happen the company cannot stand still. Instead, they always have to be trying new things and growing.

In an IT team, in order to make this kind of growth occur, innovation has to be encouraged to happen. All too often the workers on the team can get too involved in their day-to-day tasks to spend any time thinking about innovation. That's where the IT manager has to step in.

As the IT manager it is your job to create an environment in which your team that will not only encourage innovation to happen but will also help it to grow once it starts. A great deal of this has to do with how you communicate to the team what you want to happen.

Innovation is something that we all know that we want to have happen, but just exactly how to make it occur is what often eludes us. As the IT manager you are going to have to identify the innovation strategies that will work with your team and your IT department and then implement them.

It's possible that either innovation projects have been tried in the past and have not worked or, more likely, there is no innovation going on right now. It is your job to change this and make innovation take root and become part of everyone's daily routine.

This book is filled with tools that IT managers can use to introduce innovation into their teams. These ideas range from learning to grow good ideas to doing more with what you already have. No matter what approach you decide to take, the goal is the same: cause innovation to take root and grow.

Making innovation happen is not easy. By reading this book you will have the ideas and the techniques that you need to cause it to happen in your team. Once this happens, it can spread to the rest of the IT department. This is the kind of leadership that the company is looking for from their IT managers.

For more information on what it takes to be a great IT manager, check out my blog, The Accidental IT Leader, at:

www.TheAccidentalITLeader.com

Good luck!

- Dr. Jim Anderson

About The Author

I must confess that I never set out to be a CIO. When I went to school, I studied Computer Science and thought that I'd get a nice job programming and that would be that. Well, at least part of that plan worked out!

My first job was working for Boeing on their F/A-18 fighter jet program. I spent my days programming fighter jet software in assembly language and I loved it. The U.S. government decided to save some money and went looking for other countries to sell this plane to. This put me into an unfamiliar role: I started to meet with foreign military officials and I ended up having to manage groups of engineers who were working on international projects.

Time moved on and so did I. I found myself working for Siemens, the big German telecommunications company. They were making phone switches and selling them to the seven U.S. phone companies. The problem was that the switches were too complicated. Customers couldn't tell the difference between one complicated phone switch from another complicated phone switch. Once again I found myself working with the sales and marketing teams to find ways to make the great technology that the engineers had developed understandable to both internal and external customers.

I've spent over 25 years working as an senior IT professional for both big companies and startups. This has given me an opportunity to learn what it takes to manage and IT department in ways that allow it to maximize its output while becoming a valuable part of the overall company.

I now live in Tampa Florida where I spend my time managing my consulting business, Blue Elephant Consulting, teaching college courses at the University of South Florida, and traveling to work with companies like yours to share the knowledge that I have about how to create and manage successful IT departments.

I'm always available to answer questions and I can be reached at:

Dr. Jim Anderson
Blue Elephant Consulting
Email: jim@BlueElephantConsulting.com
Facebook: http://goo.gl/1TVoK
Web: **www.BlueElephantConsulting.com**

"Unforgettable communication skills that will set your ideas free..."

Create IT Departments That Are Productive And A Valuable Asset To The Rest Of The Company !

Dr. Jim Anderson is available to provide training and coaching on the topics that are the most important to people who have to manage IT departments: how can I build a productive IT department (and keep it together) while at the same time providing the rest of the company with the IT services that they need?

Dr. Anderson believes that in order to both learn and remember what he says, speakers need to laugh. Each one of his speeches is full of fun and humor so that what he says "sticks" with everyone.

Dr. Anderson's CIO SkillsTraining Includes:

1. How to identify and attract the right type of IT workers to your IT department.
2. How to build relationships with the company's senior management in order to get the support that you need?
3. How to stay on top of changing technology and security issues so that you never get surprised?

Dr. Jim Anderson works with over 100 customers per year. To invite Dr. Anderson to work with you, contact him at:

Phone: 813-418-6970 or
Email: jim@BlueElephantConsulting.com

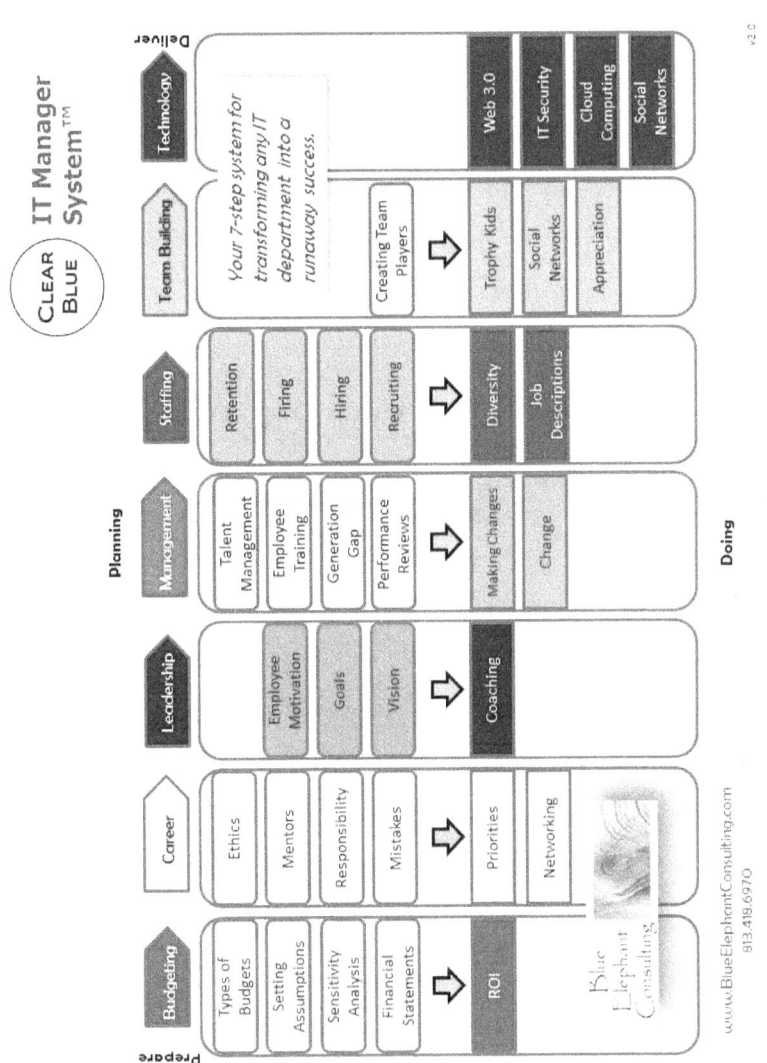

The **Clear Blue IT Manager System™** has been created to provide IT managers with a clear roadmap for how to manage an IT team. This system shows IT Managers what needs to be done and in what order to do it.

Chapter 1

Is An IT Manager Really An Artist?

Chapter 1: Is An IT Manager Really An Artist?

Here's an interesting question that I like to whip out every so often and run through my mind: is IT a science or an art? For that matter, are we all engineers or are we really artists? If you think about it, our jobs consist of taking basic elements (colors) combining them (painting) and creating networks, servers, and applications (works of art). Is one among us the next IT Michelangelo?

Ed Catmull is one of the founders of Pixar and he is currently the president of Pixar and Disney Animation Studios (they merged just a while ago). He wrote an article for the Harvard Business Review in which he discussed how Pixar deals with the mix of art and technology that they use to create their films. His thoughts hold some interesting points for us IT Leaders.

One of the first points that Catamull makes is that Disney and Pixar are not just about great artists (Walt Disney being one of them). Rather, what makes them stand out is that they have learned to take technology and bend it in such a way as to help their artists do more. Sure seems like what an IT department is supposed to be doing!

At Pixar they have a saying "Technology inspires art, and art challenges the technology". No matter what market your business operates in, this saying should apply to you also.

At Pixar they have developed several principles that they use to capture this saying and implement it in how they do work. Because every team in the department is not created equal, Pixar has implemented the following principles to guide their teams:

1. **Communication Is Key And Unrestricted**: In order to ensure that silos of information don't develop, they have separated the decision making hierarchy from the communications hierarchy. There needs to be no such thing as going through "proper channels" to get information. This means that Leaders have to get comfortable with the fact that they won't know everything and others may know more than they do.

2. **New Ideas Must Be Safe**: Nothing can kill innovation like an environment in which new ideas are laughed at or shot down. Everyone needs to get two-sided feedback: tell them what you liked and tell them what you didn't like.

3. **Good Ideas Start In School**: Oh the arrogance of those of us who have been out of school for many years. We forget where the next generation of workers will come from and where new ideas often spring from. We need to encourage our workers to publish their results, challenges, and solutions. Yes, you may end up giving away some competitive advantage but you'll get so much more back in reader feedback and attracting new talent that it will all be worth it.

Catmull took the time to point out a few additional things that Pixar has done to keep their workers communicating with each other:

- The Pixar building has been designed with the cafeteria, mailboxes, meeting rooms, and bathrooms are located in a common atrium. This was done to maximize chance encounters between coworkers. It goes without saying that this is how breakthroughs and solutions just "happen".

- When a company is successful, the ability to create a way to systematically ward off complacency while at the same time finding ways to uncover problems are probably the two most difficult issues facing a Leader.

- Postmortems are the key to your company's long term success. Nobody likes to do them, but everyone learns from them. Catmull suggests changing the format of the postmortem meeting so that people don't become complacent. He also suggests that you ask each group involved in the postmortem to create a list of the 5 things that they would do again and the 5 things that they would not do again. This creates a safer environment.

I guess at the end of the day, just like the teams at Pixar, we are all artists down deep. The tools that we use and the artwork that we create may be different from what we traditionally think of artists creating, but isn't that what art is all about?

Chapter 2

How IT Leaders Can Grow Good Ideas

Chapter 2: How IT Leaders Can Grow Good Ideas

Innovation, innovation, innovation. Everyone seems to be talking about it, but nobody seems to have any clear guidance for IT Leaders when it comes to telling them **HOW to grow good ideas** within their IT departments. Well we're going to change that starting right now.

Dr. Jan van den-Ende and Bob Kijuit have spent some time thinking about this problem and they've got some suggestions for us. The problem that they've been doing research on is just how to come up with systems that will allow IT departments to nurture **GOOD** ideas while at the same time getting rid of **BAD** ideas.

In a nutshell, what they have found is that if you can come up with a way to tap into **the input of many people** early on in the idea process, then you can make sure that the good ideas make it all the way to the top.

In most companies, new ideas are often collected via some form of the old fashion "suggestion box". Using this method, literally **thousands of ideas** can be submitted in a company of medium size if you have an enthusiastic work force. The problem that this causes is that then someone has to review all of those suggestions and identify the worthy ones. Good luck with that!

What the research has found is that if people take the time to **discuss their ideas with colleagues** then this helps out a lot. These discussions can help further refine the idea in terms of technical issues or market feasibility. If the idea is really a stinker, then it will cause it to be quickly discarded.

The researchers have also discovered two additional things:

- If ideas are discussed with colleagues who work outside of the submitter's department instead of colleagues inside his department, then there was a better chance of the idea eventually being accepted.

- If ideas were discussed with friends and trusted colleagues then once again the idea had a better chance of eventually being accepted.

The reason for these higher acceptance rates is probably because both close friends and outsiders can give the most **frank feedback**.

IT Leaders can help their departments to generate innovative ideas. They just need to introduce this **additional review and discussion step** into the process in order to improve the quality of the ideas being submitted.

Chapter 3

3 Reasons Innovation Doesn't Happen In IT

Chapter 3: 3 Reasons Innovation Doesn't Happen In IT

Welcome to the world of overused buzz words! The star of the show these days is "**innovation**" – everyone wants it, everyone is talking about it, nobody really knows how to get it. IT Leaders find themselves in a situation where if they aren't careful, they just might make one of **three different mistakes** that could prevent innovation from happening within their teams...

The Communication Problem

Researchers Rob Cross, Andrew Hargadon, Salvatore Parise, and Robert Thomas have looked into what kills innovation on a team. #1 on their list of culprits is our old friend **poor communication**.

IT Leaders already know that poor communication is a major problem. However, they may not realize just how much of an **impact** that it may be having on their attempts to foster innovation in their IT team.

The causes of poor communication **can be varied**: staff in different physical locations (even working on different floors of the same building can be a hindrance), an organizational structure that may prevent teams from talking to each other, or it could as simple as different IT Leaders being in competition with each other and not being willing to communicate.

The Roadblock Problem

It is my belief that in order to be an effective IT Leader it's as much **who** you know as **what** you know. When it comes to fostering innovation in your IT team it turns out that the same is true.

Within an IT department there are often certain people who become **experts** about one or more parts of the IT shop. This in turn puts these people in a position of power. Other IT staff must seek them out in order to get the information that they need to do their jobs or to get permission to complete some task that impacts the area under the expert's control.

Having IT experts is not a bad thing in of itself. However, when these experts are allowed to **control the flow of new ideas** problems start to arise. Often times these experts will have had experiences that will cloud the way that they see the world. This means that they may quash innovative IT ideas based on their personal experiences that would otherwise benefit the company.

The Insulated Staff Problem

As much as we like to brag about all of the workplace benefits that working in the 21st Century has brought about, our communication networks are still **amazingly frail**. When IT departments allow staff to remain insulated, innovation can flounder.

A great deal of time and effort goes into **setting up the deals** that allow IT operations and development to be outsourced to other firms. However, once those deals have been set up, the communication channels between the firms are often left in the hands of just a few people.

This means that any innovation that occurs at either firm will be hard pressed to make it through this **narrow communication channel** to the other firm. Additionally, if the person who is the conduit leaves the firm, then communication will be damaged or lost.

Final Thoughts

IT Leaders are responsible for **fostering and growing innovation** within their teams. This job is hard enough without the extra challenge of encountering additional roadblocks to innovation.

Having the ability to **recognize** the three most common obstacles to a successful innovation program is the first step in dealing with these challenges. Once an IT Leader recognizes that an innovation problem exists, then a solution can start to be crafted.

If you develop the ability to spot these three innovation blockers then you will have found a way to transform yourself from an IT manager into a **true leader**.

Chapter 4

It Takes A Village To Innovate Like An IT Department

Chapter 4: It Takes A Village To Innovate Like An IT Department

So IT Leader, what are you going to do about **boosting the innovation** within your team? Your hands are tied when it comes to giving out raises – not that money really helps innovation. You don't have any spots to offer promotions into because the company has adopted a "flat" organizational structure. Oh, and all of your workers are running around afraid that they might lose their jobs any day now. Good luck with making innovation happen here!

It's All About Words

Sure we read about big "**innovation generation**" exercises that those fancy firms put on where they haul everyone out into the woods for a week and make them climb trees together until they agree to innovate together if only they'd be allowed to return home and eat normal food once again. It turns out that as an IT Leader, you can make innovation happen within your team by doing something much simpler (and less costly).

Innovation happens when **the right person talks with the right person**. As an IT Leader it's your job to make this happen. This means that you've got to know both your team and the rest of the company. Since you know your staff, you know what their talents are. Using this information, you need to have them go out and talk with the other parts of the company where there are people with complementary talents.

Just Make A Decision Already!

If you want to kill innovation in your department, then the simplest thing that you can do is to **make it hard to get**

permission to test a new idea. All too often the decision making processes that we have in place are legacy artifacts that are left over from days gone by.

If you take a look at just what it takes in order for a fresh idea to bubble to the surface and get permission to be tested, then you'll know what needs to change. This process should have **as little friction as possible** and should be perceived as being easy to do.

Who's In Charge Here?

When it's time to come up with a new idea, the person that you appoint to run the show will be the key to its success or failure. I'm just as guilty of this as anyone but we naturally tend to **choose the best performers** in one particular area to lead the team that is in charge of innovating. It turns out that this is the wrong decision.

What we should be doing is realizing that success in this area is going to really be more dependent on connections that the leader has with other parts of the company instead of any special technical skills that they may have. This means that we need to find those team members who are the best "**hooked in**" and let them lead the team.

Come Together, Right Now...

Where people sit and who they work side-by-side with is key to their ability to come up with innovative ideas. If you insist that your team members sit in the same location or if you resist transferring people to other departments to work on a project, then **you'll be acting as a roadblock** to the very innovation that you are so desperately seeking.

Beware Of Energy Vampires

Hopefully it goes without saying that it's much easier to work with **positive people** instead of negative people. This is something that you've got to watch out for and plan around very carefully.

It can be very easy to identify those people that will enable your team to make forward progress and those that will drain both their energy and enthusiasm. Once you know this, then you've got to work to keep your team away from the "**energy vampires**" so that they'll remain highly productive.

Final Thoughts

Nobody ever said that being an IT Leader was going to be an easy job. One of your responsibilities is to make sure that your team is able to create and deliver **innovative ideas**. With little budget or other such levers, you're going to have to get creative.

Knowing that innovation is often caused by having your staff interact with others, you need to make sure that such **opportunities exist**. Simplifying decision making and ensuring that novel ideas can be tested is a good way to foster innovation. Remember that in the end, an IT team that is innovative will have the ability to solve the greatest number of business problems.

Chapter 5

Doing More With What You Already Have

Chapter 5: Doing More With What You Already Have

As an IT Leader, you've got a bit of a challenge on your hands right now. There is probably no way that you're going to be getting more funding or headcount in the immediate future (or at least not enough to make a difference).

Yet at the same time your senior management keeps talking about the need for the IT department to start showing some innovation. Sounds like you've gotten yourself into **yet another bind**. How about if we take a look at how you can exceed your expectations using what you already have…

It's All About The Information

Eric Lundquist over at eWeek magazine points out that one way for an IT team to show innovation is for it to **create new ways to leverage company information**. Two ways of doing this include taking existing company information and combining it in different ways and the other is creating new information from resources that already exist.

Within IT we all know the dirty little secret: **our systems don't talk to each other**. What this means is that we have databases that are stuffed with silos of customer, product, and operations information sprinkled throughout the company.

It does not take a genius to realize that simply by creating an application that has access to two databases that have not previously been connected an IT team can create a new information tool. By creating this type of data **"mashup"** multiple times, the innovation that has been requested can be delivered.

It's Time To Optimize

Anyone up for more layoffs? Ok, so that's not the type of optimization that we're talking about here. Any company runs by **executing processes**. IT has the ability to help optimize those processes. The first step in doing this is to measure the processes as they exist today in order to be able to determine what parts of what processes need improvement.

In the old days, this type of process measurement simply focused on people and documents. Now we realize that there's more than meets the eye here. If you look at the **full infrastructure** of what it takes to run a company and execute a process, then you need to account for things like electricity, air conditioning, physical space, etc.

Most companies that compete against each other end up with very similar processes. If your IT team can come up with a way to make your company's process better / quicker / faster than the other guy's process then **that truly would be an innovation**.

Risk Is What You Make Of It

Risk to a company comes in many forms. Most firms focus on making sure that they are complying with both state and federal regulations. Rarely does a company see risk management as an avenue to innovation and so more often than not they end up trying to do the **bare minimum** needed just to get by the regulators.

There is a different approach that you can take with your IT team. If you assign them the task of determining where the risk to the company lies, they just might surprise you with **what they come up with**. Once they've identified where the risks are, assign them to create solutions that will either minimize or eliminate these risks. You just might be surprised with the level of innovation that empowering your team creates.

What All Of This Means For You

Innovation is currently a **popular buzzword** both in business and in IT. As IT Leaders we are being asked to create innovation within our teams using the resources that we currently have available.

If we take the time to look around, we will find that we have **three opportunities** to make things happen using what our teams already have. The first is to bring silos of company data together in order to create information that doesn't currently exist. Next we have the opportunity to measure existing company processes in order to find out where IT can help optimize the processes. Finally, IT has a key role to play in minimizing the risk that the company faces and by empowering your IT team you can uncover hidden risks.

Innovation is there, you just have to take the time to uncover where it is hiding. You need to move quickly, because there's **a lot more** that your IT team needs to get done after this!

Chapter 6

How Seeing The Future Helped NCR's IT Leaders Do More

Chapter 6: How Seeing The Future Helped NCR's IT Leaders Do More

"Think outside of the box" is what IT Leaders seem to be hearing more and more every day. Well that's great advice, but how do you actually go about doing it? It turns out that IT managers over at NCR seem to have come up with a way to do this. Maybe we should all take a moment and listen to what they have to say…

The World Of Information Processing Systems

NCR (once upon a time known as National Cash Register) is a company that these days makes all sorts of electronic devices: ATM machines, data kiosks, software to run data warehouses, etc. It turns out that they are **very, very successful**.

Samuel Greengard had a chance to sit down with some NCR IT managers and find out what makes them tick. They've actually run into **a bit of a problem**: they've almost been too successful. When you can count 19 of the top 20 banks as customers for your ATM machines, you clearly have a lot of electronic products out in the field.

NCR's issue is that with that many devices out there, a **reactive approach** to handling repair and maintenance (you call, we come) just wasn't cutting it anymore. The company needed a new approach.

Out Of The Box Thinking

The IT managers who work for NCR were aware of all of the data that they had on hand. They connect to each of their products out in the field and get a steady stream of monitoring data sent back to NCR's data centers all the time. This would explain why they have **a 24PB data warehouse**.

The NCR IT managers realized that they probably had enough data on hand to start to try to **predict the future**. For example, if a particular type of ATM machine had a historical record of failing after 100,000 operations, then as this type of machine started to approach 100,000 operations, they knew that a failure was coming up.

It's really no breakthrough thought to realize that with this kind of knowledge, NCR now sends its repair teams out to service equipment in the field before they break – **sorta like seeing the future**.

Fortune Telling Equipment

Although the concept might be simple, it takes **teams of dedicated IT staffers** to make it happen. Specifically, although NCR has reams of data on their deployed equipment, turning this sea of information into usable knowledge requires some serious IT horsepower.

Very large storage systems, ultra-fast servers, and complex algorithms are required to make sense of it all. However, the value that the IT teams are bringing to the table doesn't stop there. NCR field technicians now carry **Blackberrys** that are used to tell them where to go next. The NCR IT managers have just about automated the whole process.

What This Means For You

Just making sure that servers stay up and that the company's email system is available is no longer enough for an IT team to do. **Innovative thinking** is required in order to find ways for the

IT department to help the rest of the company compete in the global marketplace.

Over at NCR their IT managers have found ways to **leverage their IT systems** and data in order to boost customer satisfaction. By mining data collected from customer equipment and running it through IT systems, NCR's IT managers have been able to predict when equipment will need service so that outages can be prevented.

Novel thinking is nothing new in IT teams. However, applying that thinking to finding ways that the company can **move faster and do more** is what IT Leaders need to be doing these days.

Chapter 7

The Reason That Innovation Isn't Happening In Your IT Team

Chapter 7: The Reason That Innovation Isn't Happening In Your IT Team

How many times do you have to tell your team: it's time to start innovating again? The global recession is over, if your part of the IT department is going to start to grow and be successful, then your team is going to have to be out in front and leading the charge. Since budgets are still constrained, it's going to take a great deal of innovation to find ways to do more with what you currently have. Why isn't anyone doing this?

You Are Not Alone

I'm not sure if this is going to make you feel any better, but as an IT Team Leader you are not alone in this absence of innovation. Lots of IT teams are finding that they are missing that spark of innovation also.

What's going on here? That's the very question that two researchers, Feirong Yuan and Richard Woodman , set out to answer. They sent out surveys to 100's of employees of companies and they covered everyone from the top of the pyramid to the folks doing the coding.

It's All About Image

Their findings were actually quite interesting. What they discovered is that innovation in an IT team is being withheld because team members are concerned about the risk to their workplace image that being seen as being innovative would cause. The power of creating unfavorable social impressions with their coworkers is what is keeping their mouths shut.

A lot of this can be tied back to just exactly what a given IT worker's job title is. If it doesn't explicitly say "innovator" in their job description, then you've got a problem. Team members who are not expected to be innovators feel that their coworkers will develop a negative impression of them if they start to suggest different ways of doing things.

This goes even one step further. The researchers discovered that many IT team members fear that too much innovation on their part will start to "provoke anger" among their fellow IT coworkers. This will be especially true with those workers who are happy with the way that things are – they have the "don't rock the boat" mentality.

The Role Of The IT Leader

As the IT Leader, it's going to be your job to make innovation happen in your IT team. If you don't, then you won't be an IT Leader for very long. What you are going to have to communicate to the entire team is that the whole IT department is behind the push for more innovation.

Showing that innovation is what is being expected will go a long way in setting the stage for your team. Telling the team over and over again that you are looking for them to be innovative will serve to lower the perceived social risk of coming forward with innovative suggestions.

Your job as an IT Leader is to create an IT workplace where your team will feel comfortable in being innovative. This means that you are going to have to make everyone understand that individual differences are not only tolerated, but are actually critical in order to help the team look at problems in different ways.

What All Of This Means For You

As an IT Leader you are going to have to make the most out of the resources that you have – funding will always be tight. This means that you are going to have to find ways to get your IT team to get creative and innovate. However, recent studies have shown that workers who are not expected to be innovative often worry about their image and don't speak up.

In order to change this, as an IT Leader you are going to have to clearly and repeatedly communicate to the team that innovation is not only encouraged, but it is also expected. You're going to have to create an environment in which all workers feel comfortable speaking up and being innovative.

There is no one magic action that you can take to make your team be more innovative. However, given time and a consistent message from you that innovation is a good thing, you can convince everyone in your team to think hard and become the innovation engine that the IT department is going to need in order to both survive and thrive.

Chapter 8

How IT Managers Can Bring Innovation To Their IT Teams

Chapter 8: How IT Managers Can Bring Innovation To Their IT Teams

"Be more innovative" – how many times has your management told you that? Although being innovative isn't really part of the IT Manager's job definition, IT Managers still want their IT teams to always be staying **ahead of what their internal customers want**.

We'd like to be able to have our team be solving problems that our customers might not even know that they have. However, it turns out that being innovative is very hard to do. Good news – I've got three ways that an IT Manager can capture some of that innovation stuff and apply it to their IT team.

Say Hello To Scenarios

What is innovation? I think that we can all agree that true innovation is when members of an IT team **have a breakthrough idea** about how to make a process or a service even better. The challenge is for you to take on the leadership challenge to find ways to boost the probability that someone on the IT team will have one of these ideas.

One way to make this happen is to take the time to **create scenarios**. Scenarios are very detailed written views of what the future may look like for your customers. The goal here is to make it so that the reader of the scenario can actually picture themselves in the future that is being described.

This level of detail will allow members of your IT team to "become" the customer and to experience the future. This will allow them to **experience what the customer will experience** and may lead them to having a breakthrough innovation idea.

Use That Internet Thing

Yes, someone on your IT team may have an innovative idea. However, what are you going to do **if they don't?**

It stands to reason that if you had **more people on your IT team**, then the chances of someone having a breakthrough innovative idea would be that much greater. It turns out that by using the power of the Internet, you can increase the size of your team.

When your IT team is faced with a challenge that only innovative thinking can help to solve, **turn to the Internet**. Ask for help and offer a prize or cash for the winning submission. You'll be amazed at how many submissions you get and it just might turn out that the innovative idea that you were looking for was out there – all you had to do was to ask.

Have Your Power Users Show You The Way

Not all users of your team's IT products and services are created the same. For every product there is one category of users, **the power users**, who are innovators when it comes to using your product.

This type of user is not satisfied. The current product is **not meeting their needs** and so they are being driven to use it in ways that you had not anticipated. This is where innovation can happen.

What you need to do as an IT manager is to identify these types of users. Then you need to reach out to them and find out more about what types of problems they are trying to solve. Once you understand this, take a look at how they are using your product. You just might be surprised at what you discover – they might be using your product **in innovative new ways**.

What All Of This Means For You

Yes, all of us IT managers would like to find a way to harness some innovation and apply it to the products and services that our IT team is delivering in order to **make it more successful**. However, the hard part is trying to understand just exactly how to make this happen.

One way to set yourself up to make innovation happen for your IT team is to **take the time** to create detailed scenarios of how your customers go about doing their jobs both today and in the future. You can also use the Internet to reach out to people outside of your company and enlist them to see if they can provide solutions to problems that you've not been able to solve. Finally, current power users of your products and services may have the ability to tap into the innovation energy that you are looking to find.

Innovation is not something that an IT manager can go online and buy. Instead, it's something that **just seems to happen**. This means that as an IT manager if you want it to happen for your product you need to set the stage. Follow these three suggestions and you just might be surprised at how quickly innovation transforms your IT team.

Chapter 9

How IT Managers Can Find The Innovation That Their IT Teams Need

Chapter 9: How IT Managers Can Find The Innovation That Their IT Teams Need

It seems as though our senior management is always telling us to "be more innovative" In all honesty, this was never a part of our formal job description; however, it appears as though it has been added now! IT Managers still want their IT teams to find ways to be innovative and be able to get more done with the resources that they have now.

We'd like to be able to have our team be solving problems that our customers might not even know that they have. However, it turns out that being innovative is very hard to do. I've got three ways that an IT Manager can capture some of that innovation stuff and apply it to their IT team.

Dive Deep With Your Customers

Where can an IT manager **look for innovative ideas**? One of the best places is to have the customers that your team serves provide you with the innovation insights that you are looking for.

The trick is finding a way to allow your customers to **communicate these ideas to you**. One way to go about doing this is to perform what is called a "deep dive" with your customers.

Take the time to immerse yourself into the lives of your customers. The results of doing this can include the uncovering of unserved or underserved areas. It can also provide you with information on new directions and new frames with which to search for innovative ideas to apply to your product.

Probe Your Customers

As though a deep dive wasn't enough, you can take things one step further. You can create and execute what is called **a probe-and-learn strategy** with the people who receive and use what your IT team produces. This is the kind of approach that IT managers use to find out more about areas where their products are not either active or strong in.

When you are executing a probe, what you'll actually be doing is **trying out new ideas in a new context**. The most important thing to realize about probes is that they don't always work out. A high failure rate is to be expected; however, you need to make sure that you learn something new from every probe that you try.

Look Internally

Innovation happens **when someone has a great idea**. What this means is that the more people that you are able to enlist into helping you search for innovative ideas, the better your chances are that innovation will happen for your product.

One way to boost your chances of identifying an innovative idea is to **enlist other people who work at your company to help you out**. This can be as simple as asking employees in the finance, sales, or even the procurement departments to keep their eyes open and let you know about trends that they encounter that may relate to the types of products and services that your IT team creates. This can be a great way to become aware of things that would normally go unnoticed.

What All Of This Means For You

Every IT manager would like their team to be **more innovative**, but exactly how to go about making this happen is something that too many of us struggle with. It turns out that it's not hard to do once you know how.

Three different ways to make innovation happen for your IT team include diving deep and really getting to know how your customer is using your product. You can build on this information and create probe projects that try out innovative new ideas with the expectation that most will fail, but all will produce good learning opportunities. Finally, you can tap into the power of your in-house staff: put their minds to work on how the products and services that your team creates can be more innovative.

Everything is possible; the trick is in finding out **how to make it happen for your product**. Take the time to investigate these three suggestions and see if you can use them to add some innovation to your IT team's output in order to make it even more successful!

Chapter 10

3 Steps IT Managers Can Take To Make Innovation Happen For Their Team

Chapter 10: 3 Steps IT Managers Can Take To Make Innovation Happen For Their Team

If there is one word that is in danger of being overused in the world of IT these days, it would "innovation". Our management is telling us that they want more of it, but who among us knows how to make that happen?

We'd like to be able to have our team be solving problems that our customers might not even know that they have. However, it turns out that being innovative is very hard to do. Good news – I've got three ways that an IT Manager can capture some of that innovation stuff and apply it to their IT team.

Ignite The Entrepreneur Spirit

Making innovation happen within an IT team is all about getting the individual members of the team to start to think in different ways. What can get overlooked all too often by IT managers is that this kind of thinking requires time.

In order to allow innovative thinking to occur, you need to free up your IT team to spend time thinking in innovative ways. Lots of companies such as Google and 3M have formalized programs to do this. They allocate a percentage of their staff's time (ranging from 15% to 20%) to work on project of their own choosing.

You may not be able to let your IT team free up that much of their time; however, any time that you can allow them to use to work on projects of their own choosing can only help to drive innovation. Simply showing your commitment to allowing them to be innovative will sometimes be enough to light the spark of innovation.

It's All About Words

Just exactly where does an innovation start? We'd like to think that it first shows up as a flash of insight in the mind of a solitary worker. However, more often than not it really gets its start as the result of a conversation between two workers. Someone says something that gets the other person thinking and things take off from there.

As an IT manager, you need to figure out a way to make sure that these types of conversations happen more often. One of the best sources for innovation causing conversations is when members of your IT team talk with people from different departments.

Depending on the size and the layout of your company, it can be difficult to set things up so that these types of conversations occur. However, thanks to online tools such as web sites and knowledge repositories, it is possible for members of different departments to interact and share ideas with a little bit of effort.

You're Not Like Me

Finally, people who are similar to other people have very little to say to each other – they already know what the other person is thinking. As an IT manager, you need to make sure that the IT team doesn't find itself in this kind of rut.

One way to make sure that this doesn't happen is to make sure that the people who are on the IT team are diverse. They may all look the same, but you want them to have different ways of looking at the world and different ways of thinking.

Reaching outside of the company to get in contact with teams that have different jobs or different outlooks can also help.

Hospital emergency room teams have talked with racing team pit crews in order to better understand how more can be done in less time. Your IT team could probably talk with a team from another industry to gain similar insights.

What All Of This Means For You

Every IT manager would like their team to be **more innovative**, but exactly how to go about making this happen is something that too many of us struggle with. It turns out that it's not hard to do once you know how.

As an IT manager, it's your job to find ways to ignite the spirit of innovation within your team. One great way to make this happen is to provide the members of your team with the opportunity to talk with people who work outside of IT in other parts of the company. The trick to making innovation happen within IT is to make sure that your team is made up of people who are as diverse as possible in order to look at problems differently.

Everything is possible, the trick is in finding out **how to make it happen for your team**. Take the time to investigate these three suggestions and see if you can use them to add some innovation to your IT team's output in order to make it even more successful!

Chapter 11

How Can IT Managers Be Innovative?

Chapter 11: How Can IT Managers Be Innovative?

On top of all of those budgeting and staffing things that you have to do each and every day, your company is pushing you to become more innovative. Oh great, and just how is an IT manager supposed to go about doing this?

Being innovative can be very hard to do if you don't know how to do it. The first step in pulling this off is making sure that you understand what true innovation looks like.

Don't Try To Please Everyone

Innovation is all about doing new things. We are expected to be able to do the things that will help our IT team to be successful.

Generally speaking, people don't associate "new" with an IT manager. However, the world in which we work in is constantly changing. If you don't innovate and do new and different things, then **you run the real risk of being left behind**.

One of the biggest challenges that you are going to run into when you try out new things will be the doubters that you encounter. As an IT manager, you interact with your management, your team, and the other departments that your team works with. Not everyone is going to understand what you are up to and they won't be supportive. You've got to respect their doubts and then push on – **don't let them hold you back**.

The good news here is that you are not alone. As you try out new approaches to old problems, you are traveling a well-worn path. Innovation is what made Thomas Edison, Steve Jobs, and Jeff Bezos successful. Yes, we all know who they are today, but back in the day **they were just managers who were willing to try out something new**.

Where Does Innovation Come From?

Hopefully we can all agree that innovation is a good thing. Now the big question is **just exactly where does the innovation that drives us actually come from?** Is this something that only some of us have or is it really inside of every IT manager?

The good news is that I believe that the ability to be innovative is inside of everyone. You just need to **have the courage** to look inside of yourself and find it. At its core, innovation is that part of us that allows us to act like a rebel. We are rebelling against how things currently are. We have to be willing to challenge the status quo in a quest for something better.

Innovation is not designed to make people feel good. Instead, as you innovate it's going to end up **making a lot of other people quite uncomfortable** – innovation is all about change after all. Innovation is all about evolving and doing things that have not been done before. This is going to get you noticed. You'll be charting a new path and inviting others to follow you no matter what the doubters might be saying.

What Does All Of This Mean For You?

The need to innovate is only now being recognized as **a key to a company's long-term success**. What this means is that more and more IT managers are being asked to be more innovative as they go about doing their jobs.

In order to be successful at the innovation game, **you are going to have to learn to do things differently**. The first thing that you are going to have to realize is that you won't be able to please everyone. As you innovate, various people are going to believe that you are making mistakes – ignore them. You'll also have to understand where innovation comes from. It turns out that the best innovation comes from the IT managers who are willing to be rebels and who are willing to defy the norm.

Yes, your company wants you to innovate. However, they never told you that it was going to be so difficult to do! Innovation is hard work. However, it turns out that that is ok because what innovation can produce is **so valuable that it makes all of that hard work well worth the effort**. Take the time to think about how you can bring more innovation to your IT manager job and you'll be richly rewarded for your efforts.

Chapter 12

What If Another IT Manager Just Copied Your Great Innovative Idea?

Chapter 12: What If Another IT Manager Just Copied Your Great Innovative Idea?

As an IT manager, you are always looking to create innovative ways to do your job. If you can come up with new or different ways for your team to get their work done, then there is a good chance that your management will notice you and either a raise, a promotion, or both will be coming your way.

However, we don't live and work in a vacuum – there is always the chance that just when you've come up with a great new idea, **another IT manager at your company may roll out the same innovation with their team**. What's an IT manager to do?

No Ideas Are Original

"Hey, he / she stole my idea" Well, actually not. **There are really no new ideas**. What happens is that we all have a set of circumstances and events that we encounter and our minds process them and all of sudden we have a break-through idea.

What we need to understand is that while we are doing all of this, everyone else is out there **having their own set of experiences** and, more often than we'd care to admit, having their very own personal break-through ideas. It's only natural that every so often our novel ideas will be very similar to their novel ideas.

Having the idea is not the big deal. What is going to matter is **how you go about implementing your great idea**. Another IT manager may have had the same idea, but they'll probably implement it differently than you will.

Differences Do Matter

So let's say that the worst thing imaginable has happened: just as you get ready to implement your brand-new idea, you discover that **another IT manager is doing the exact same thing**. Hold on, they are NOT doing the exactly the same thing.

Yes, yes – they may be doing something that is similar to what you are doing, but **it is not exactly the same**. What this means for you is that you now have some homework to do. You are going to have to figure out what the differences between what you are planning on doing and what they are doing will be.

Remember, the key to making your solution stand out is to take the time to **highlight what makes it different**. This can be your attitude, the humor that you and your team bring to the table, the tools that you use, or how you interact with your end customers. Once you find out what makes your solution different, build on it and make it stand out.

Keep A Close Watch

This is a delicate issue. Yes, you should keep an eye on that other IT manager. Since they are trying to implement a solution that is very similar to yours, any problems or challenges that they run into are ones that you'll probably encounter. **Watch and learn**.

However, **don't watch them too closely**. What you are going to be doing is unique. You don't want to just copy what they are doing or you'll run the risk of implementing a duplicate of their solution.

What you are going to want to do is to **find new insights and new ideas**. Once you do this, you can work them into your solution and you will have done something that is very different from what the other IT manager has done.

It's All About Competition

It can be all too easy to focus on that other IT manager and to try to create a solution that outshines him or her. However, you really need to keep an eye on the big picture. Your team's biggest competition may not be coming from your direct competition, but rather **from indirect sources**.

When you keep your eyes open and understand that the solution that your team is putting in place may be made obsolete by other factors, then you'll be able to **get inspiration from other sources**. Learn from other projects that are going on and see if you can apply any of their insights to your solution in order to make it even better.

What All Of This Means For You

IT managers are always looking for better, faster ways to get their team's work done. Sometimes it involves implementing new and innovative ideas. All too often, just when you've come up with **an innovative idea** for how your team can accomplish more, some other IT manager will have the same idea. Should you just throw your hands up and walk away?

The answer is, of course, no. Instead you need to realize no idea that you've had was never really unique.

Of course other people were going to have similar ideas. Realize that **how you were planning on implementing your idea** is different from how the other manager has done it.

Your way may be better. Don't get too focused on the other IT manager – keep coming up with new ideas. Finally, don't get too focused on trying to beat other IT manager, make sure that you are still meeting your end customer's needs.

Innovation is a tricky thing. We all think that we are the only ones who can come up with the next "killer idea".

In truth, other people are having their own great ideas all the time. When someone else has an idea that is similar to yours, **go ahead with your idea and discover how it is different from the other IT manager's idea**.

Remember, your company needs a lot of innovation in order to be successful and your idea is part of what is going to make them be more successful!

It's from the forge of failure that the steel of success is formed.

Hard Work Does Not Guarantee Success, But Success Does Not Happen Without Hard Work.

- Dr. Jim Anderson

Create IT Departments That Are Productive And A Valuable Asset To The Rest Of The Company !

Dr. Jim Anderson is available to provide training and coaching on the topics that are the most important to people who have to manage IT departments: how can I build a productive IT department (and keep it together) while at the same time providing the rest of the company with the IT services that they need?

Dr. Anderson believes that in order to both learn and remember what he says, speakers need to laugh. Each one of his speeches is full of fun and humor so that what he says "sticks" with everyone.

Dr. Anderson's CIO SkillsTraining Includes:

1. How to identify and attract the right type of IT workers to your IT department.
2. How to build relationships with the company's senior management in order to get the support that you need?
3. How to stay on top of changing technology and security issues so that you never get surprised?

Dr. Jim Anderson works with over 100 customers per year. To invite Dr. Anderson to work with you, contact him at:

Phone: 813-418-6970 or
Email: jim@BlueElephantConsulting.com

Photo Credits:

Cover - By: elle-catraz
http://www.flickr.com/photos/elle-catraz/

Chapter 1 - By: Andrew Black
http://www.flickr.com/photos/andrewb47/

Chapter 2 - By: Brandon Cripps
http://www.flickr.com/photos/brandoncripps/

Chapter 3 - By: ImageMD
http://www.flickr.com/photos/imagemd/

Chapter 4 - By: Allan Hopkins
http://www.flickr.com/photos/hoppy1951/

Chapter 5 - By: James Bowe
http://www.flickr.com/photos/jamesrbowe/

Chapter 6 - By: Nellyfus
http://www.flickr.com/photos/nellyfus/

Chapter 7 - By: Sergio Alvarez
http://www.flickr.com/photos/tranchis/

Chapter 8 - By: Vahid
http://www.flickr.com/photos/el_chupacabrito/

Chapter 9 - By: Austin Gruenweller
http://www.flickr.com/photos/three_sixteen/

Chapter 10 - By: Paul Downey
http://www.flickr.com/photos/psd/

Chapter 11 - By: Dan Mason
http://www.flickr.com/photos/masondan/

Chapter 12 - By: Christian Guthier
http://www.flickr.com/photos/wheatfields/

Other Books By The Author

Product Management

- Product Management Secrets: Techniques For Product Managers To Boost Product Sales And Increase Customer Satisfaction

- Product Development Lessons For Product Managers: How Product Managers Can Create Successful Products

- Customer Lessons For Product Managers: Techniques For Product Managers To Better Understand What Their Customers Really Want

- Product Failure Lessons For Product Managers: Examples Of Products That Have Failed For Product Managers To Learn From

- Communication Skills For Product Managers: The Communication Skills That Product Managers Need To Know How To Use In Order To Have A Successful Product

- How To Have A Successful Product Manager Career: The Things That You Need To Be Doing TODAY In Order To Have A Successful Product Manager Career

- Product Manager Product Success: How to keep your product on track and make it become a success

Public Speaking

- How To Give A Great Presentation: Presentation techniques that will transform a speech into a memorable event

- How To Rehearse In Order To Give The Perfect Speech: How to effectively rehearse your next speech to that your message be remembered forever!

- Secrets To Creating The Perfect Speech: How to create a speech that will make your message be remembered forever!

- Secrets To Organizing The Perfect Speech: How to organize the best speech of your life!

- Secrets To Planning The Perfect Speech: How to plan to give the best speech of your life

- How To Show What You Mean During A Presentation: How to use visual techniques to transform a speech into a memorable event

<u>CIO Skills</u>

- What CIOs Need To Know About Working With Partners: Techniques For CIOs To Use In Order To Be Able To Successfully Work With Partners

- Critical CIO Management Skills: Decision Making Skills That Every CIO Needs To Have In Order To Be Able To Make The Right Choices

- How CIOs Can Make Innovation Happen: Tips And Techniques For CIOs To Use In Order To Make Innovation Happen In Their IT Department

- CIO Communication Skills Secrets: Tips And Techniques For CIOs To Use In Order To Become Better Communicators

- Managing Your CIO Career: Steps That CIOs Have To Take In Order To Have A Long And Successful Career

- CIO Business Skills: How CIOs can work effectively with the rest of the company!

IT Manager Skills

- Staffing Skills IT Managers Must Have: Tips And Techniques That IT Managers Can Use In Order To Correctly Staff Their Teams

- Secrets Of Effective Leadership For IT Managers: Tips And Techniques That IT Managers Can Use In Order To Develop Leadership Skills

- IT Manager Career Secrets: Tips And Techniques That IT Managers Can Use In Order To Have A Successful Career

- IT Manager Budgeting Skills: How IT Managers Can Request, Manage, Use, And Track Their Funding

Negotiating

- Learn The Skill Of Exploring In A Negotiation: How To Develop The Skill Of Exploring What Is Possible In A Negotiation In Order To Reach The Best Possible Deal

- Learn How To Argue In Your Next Negotiation: How To Develop The Skill Of Effective Arguing In A Negotiation In Order To Get The Best Possible Outcome

- How To Open Your Next Negotiation: How To Start A Negotiation In Order To Get The Best Possible Outcome

- Preparing For Your Next Negotiation: What You Need To Do BEFORE A Negotiation Starts In Order To Get The Best Possible Deal

<u>Miscellaneous</u>

- Power Distribution Unit (PDU) Secrets: What Everyone Who Works In A Data Center Needs To Know!

- Making The Jump: How To Land Your Dream Job When You Get Out Of College!

"Tips And Techniques For IT Managers To Use In Order To Make Innovation Happen In Their Teams"

> This book has been written with one goal in mind – to show you how you bring the spirit of innovation into your IT team. It's not easy being an IT manager so we're going to show you the strategies and techniques that you can use to introduce the spark of innovation in your team!
>
> **Let's Make Your IT Career A Success!**

What You'll Find Inside:

- **HOW IT LEADERS CAN GROW GOOD IDEAS**

- **3 REASONS INNOVATION DOESN'T HAPPEN IN IT**

- **IT TAKES A VILLAGE TO INNOVATE LIKE AN IT DEPARTMENT**

- **3 STEPS IT MANAGERS CAN TAKE TO MAKE INNOVATION HAPPEN FOR THEIR TEAM**

Dr. Jim Anderson brings his 25 years of real-world experience to this book. He's been an IT manager at some of the world's largest firms. He's going to show you what you need to do (and not do!) in order to successfully manage your career!

www.ingramcontent.com/pod-product-compliance
Lightning Source LLC
Chambersburg PA
CBHW071804170526
45167CB00003B/1171